The Evolution of the Feminine Soul

~ a transformational journal for women awakening to the Feminine

Leonor Murciano-Luna, PhD

Copyright (c) 2018 Dr. Leonor Murciano-Luna

ALL RIGHTS RESERVED. No part of this book publication may be reproduced, stored in a retrieval system, or transmitted in any form or by any means, electronic, mechanical, photocopy, recording, or any other, except brief quotation in reviews, without the prior permission of the author or publisher.

Printed in the United States of America
First Printing, 2018
ISBN-13: 978-0-692-69902-7
Nuralight Publishing
ConsciousFeminineMedicine.com

Awakening to the 13 pillars of the Conscious Feminine within you

Welcome to your Lunar Transformational Journey, as She awakens you to the Conscious Feminine. You are embarking on a process of transformation, remembrance, awakening and ultimately the evolution of your Feminine Soul.

This is an opportunity to awaken to the Feminine as you embark on a 30 day Lunar Journey with Her, while reflecting on the 13 pillars of the Conscious Feminine.

Throughout the pages of this journal, "Evolution of your Feminine Soul', you will become aware of how the Feminine is rising within you... but most importantly you will begin to remember your own forgotten Truth.

This is the transformation of awakening.

As you read each page, take the time to be present with the awareness and wisdom that arise within you in response. A space has been provided for you to journal your thoughts, epiphanies and 'aha' moments as you read each page and contemplate the reflection questions.

In reality, your Being already knows the Truth that you are about to read on these pages, however, sometimes we may need a catalyst to break through the illusory veils that have kept it hidden from our consciousness.

Let this be your catalyst, supporting the evolution of your Feminine Soul.

~ evolution of the Feminine Soul

Welcoming the Return of my Feminine Soul

The time has come to

awaken and realize the

Truth of my Being...

The Truth that I Am magnificent beyond belief.

The time is here to break out of the

spell of limitation and separation,

and detach from my

limited, separated identity.

This is the time to

realize the wholeness of my divinity.

I welcome the

evolution of my Feminine Soul.

~ evolution of the Feminine Soul

Entering the evolution of the Feminine Soul

We are in the awakening times following the 2012 global shift of consciousness. This emergence brings with it the expansion of beauty, love and compassion that we carry in our hearts and in our soul. However in order to begin manifesting that on our planet, we must begin to see beyond the veils of separation, pain and suffering.

What we focus on expands, therefore focusing on our light, rather than the chaos that is accompanying this shift, is imperative, as we continue to discover our own sacred power. The tides are changing, we are poised at the edge of the cliff. Collectively, the door is now open to manifest our greatest light, within ourselves and on our planet.

~ evolution of the Feminine Soul

Truth of the evolution of the Feminine Soul

Many of us feel an unwavering need growing in our being to do more and to be of service for the greater good, at this time. We feel a calling, a deep sense of yearning to awaken to greater love. This is the inspiration of the Conscious Feminine expressing through you. There is no question that She is growing the seeds of enlightenment and greatness in our hearts, even though we may only see the shadows of darkness in the preceding chaos.

We may even feel the potential of a new world rising within us, and the desire to dive deeper into our transformational journey of becoming that which we want to see in the outer world. There is no doubt that the new era is afoot.

Can you feel Her presence within you?

~ evolution of the Feminine Soul

Embracing the evolution of the Feminine Soul

The era is now, and we are the dreamers, dreaming into existence the reality of the Feminine. We have one assignment, and that is the awakening of Truth, in service to the evolution of the Feminine soul, within ourselves and our planet.

For the last 5000-8000 years we have lived with the concepts and perception of the FATHER GOD; of the masculine as our Divine, while the Feminine has been in obscurity. Now the Feminine is being resurrected, in order to bring the grace and harmony needed for the realization of the greatest phase of our evolutionary existence, where we are able to realize our union of both divine and human beings.

Can you hear the call of the Feminine?

~ evolution of the Feminine Soul

Sacredness of the evolution of the Feminine Soul

In the evolutionary process of the Feminine Soul, we are able to restore the consciousness of the Feminine in our Being, in our psyches and in our life. As the Feminine becomes conscious within us... we return to our innate embodiment of compassion, love, intuition, joyfulness, bliss and visceral womb wisdom that has been lost, along with Her.

As we reestablish the great Feminine within us, we, as women realize the sacredness in our bodies, we remember our union with the Divine and the secret sacredness of our wombs.

~ evolution of the Feminine Soul

Unity of the evolution of the Feminine Soul

In this evolutionary process of the Feminine Soul we are able to merge the Conscious Feminine with the Divine Masculine, creating the unity within ourselves and our planet. It is time to unveil the ancient, hidden wisdom secrets and allow them to rise through us, as we restore ourselves as vessels of greater consciousness.

Women are poised at the forefront of this evolution, as this ancient wisdom enters our womb, where it undergoes the spiritual alchemy of giving birth to a whole new creation within ourselves and our planet. This new creation is a non-dual level of consciousness emerging within ourselves as we awaken to the oneness inherent in the duality of Heaven and Earth, masculine and feminine, yin and yang...

This is the next step in our evolution towards perfected human beings.

Can you feel the realm of possibilities within you?

~ evolution of the Feminine Soul

Sacred Initiation of
the evolution of the Feminine Soul

The feminine soul collectively and personally is poised at the door of initiation, awaiting its evolutionary process of our own personal transformation. This initiatory process heals the unconscious wounds of separation that we have collectively experienced in the last 5000-8000 years. While this collective experience has affected men as well as women, it is women, that need to deeply heal their own Feminine Soul, in order to birth of new state of consciousness and lead the way. The evolution of the Feminine soul in women happens through the awakening of Truths that have been hidden under layers of judgement, shame, and fear.

The *13 pillars of Conscious Feminine Medicine* offers a map to embody these secret teachings and alchemize them in your being, transforming the layers of unconscious pain and suffering, we have been buying into.

Conscious Feminine Medicine encompasses the Sacred Initiations of the Feminine, which transforms the 3 collective wounds of the Feminine within each woman.

All you have to do is say YES, to your greatest potential of Light.

~ evolution of the Feminine Soul

Yearning for the evolution of your Feminine Soul

Perhaps you have always felt a great sense of destiny within yourself. Many souls have incarnated at this time to activate the manifestation of our greatest potential as human beings, here on Earth. Perhaps, the spiritual world has been calling you and you have heard the faint whispers of your soul's yearning urging you to make a difference in this world. First, we unleash the great compassion and love of our divine nature within us, then we become conduits and transmitters in the field of LOVE, throughout the world. We have lived in the inner worlds of Her mystery and we can feel it is time to finally come out and be the healer in our world. The Feminine is being birthed through each one of us, manifesting a world of compassion and love.

Are you willing to embrace your Divine Nature of LOVE, and stand in the full power of the Conscious Feminine within in you, now?

~ evolution of the Feminine Soul

Transformation of the evolution of the Feminine Soul

Despite the outer appearance of our world, change is here and we are beginning to see the rise of the Feminine everywhere! As we believe in the Feminine within us, we begin to believe in the realm of possibilities that are waiting to be birthed. This is key to the manifestation of LOVE on our planet.

Oneness reality is the foundational Truth of everything, however, it needs you to become conscious to it, in order to be manifested in our world.

Now is the time to step into the full realization of your being, awakening to all the aspects of Her within you. By doing so, Love dissolves the pain and suffering of the past and expands through the evolutionary impulse of the Conscious Feminine.

Are you ready to envision a new possibility in your world?

~ evolution of the Feminine Soul

Emergence of the Conscious Feminine, as we embody the 13 Pillars of Conscious Feminine Medicine

Following are the *13 pillars of Conscious Feminine Medicine*, which are composed of the structures (masculine forces) through which the Essence of the Conscious Feminine (feminine) can be born again through us. Each pillar of the Conscious Feminine Medicine represents the evolutionary process of the Feminine soul collectively and personally.

Contemplate and reflect on each pillar as your read it. Slow down enough to feel these TRUTHS resonating within your being and your body. Write the reflections that awaken within you with your own words on these pages.

Returning to the Rhythm of the Moon

As you begin your journey, take pause and notice where the Moon is in the sky, and journal the reflections that arise while you join Her, cycling through the expansion and contraction of Her monthly dance.

~ evolution of the Feminine Soul

The Waxing Phase of the Moon

For the first half of her cycle, 15 days, the moon will grow her light fuller with each day, culminating in a beautiful radiant expansion vision of Her body. Journey with Her, reflecting on her wisdom words, as you explore the 13 pillars of Conscious Feminine Medicine.

~ evolution of the Feminine Soul

First Pillar:
Women as Healers

Deep within the *Womb* of the women, the primordial blueprint of Life- unconditional Love, is woven into its very fabric. It is birthed into form, from generation to generation. This primordial *Essence* of Love bridges the world of unseen and seen. Through the womb, women give birth to the next generation, manifesting light into form.

As you cultivate greater light in your being by healing collective and personal wounds; you synergistically raise the consciousness of light being birthed on the planet. In this way, you are a natural Healer, acting as a vessel for transformational alchemy of Light to flow through you.

How are you honoring your Healership ability as a Woman?

~ evolution of the Feminine Soul

~ evolution of the Feminine Soul

New Moon Day 1
Waxing Crescent Lunar Journey

My Feminine Lunar Cycle Begins Anew

~ evolution of the Feminine Soul

Second Pillar
You are the Medicine

The medicine is contained within us all. That which we seek on the outer to bring us joy, happiness and contentment is rooted in the inner planes of our Essence. Here, we carry the medicine for that which our hearts yearn. We are the ones we have been waiting for.

As humans, there is an internal need to seek fulfillment, joy and happiness. While most of us spend our time looking for that fulfillment out there, we do not realize that the outer world appears in its form as a mirror of our inner world. Thus, fulfillment and happiness does not come from a fleeting moment in the outer world, the outer world is forever changing forms. The happiness that we are looking for is within... this is where we find the true medicine of contentment... by embodying our relationship with our Essence of Love, source of all.

Can you feel the Medicine of your Being, residing in your core?

~ evolution of the Feminine Soul

~ evolution of the Feminine Soul

Day 2
Waxing Crescent Lunar Journey

I Feel the Impulse of Her, within Me

~ evolution of the Feminine Soul

Third Pillar
Greatest Potential to Heal is Within

What we see on the outer levels of our being is a physical manifestation of the conditioned stories of our perceptual reality. Therefore, addressing our struggles through outer fixes, limits us to the creation of mind and perception without truly changing the unconscious, limiting stories we have mistaken as Truth. We contain the ability to heal through the activation of our core nature of Divine Essence.

Essence of Truth, Oneness, dissolves all other forms of non-truths and vibratory states that create pain and suffering through the dissolution of the veils of calcified patterns of survival. You are not a victim of life, but rather contain the secret coding to activate the true healing.

Let yourself reflect on your body's ability to heal itself, through the activation of the Light that you are. What does that feel like?

~ evolution of the Feminine Soul

~ evolution of the Feminine Soul

Day 3
Waxing Crescent Lunar Journey

I Invite the Realm of All Possibilities

~ evolution of the Feminine Soul

Fourth Pillar
Unveiling your Trinity Womb

We carry the *Trinity Womb* of Creative Expression, Love, and Wisdom. The 3 Wombs can be accessed through our head, heart and sacral womb area. The worlds of spirituality and matter are not separate, but interwoven... and our physical form the a densest form of spiritual Essence manifesting through these three wombs.

Our *Head Womb* is our womb of thinking and sensing;
allowing our expression of creative thoughts in the world.

Our *Heart Womb* transmits the frequencies
of Love and other emotional states.

Our *Sacral Womb* is our womb of Essence...
where we receive wisdom and merge with the Infinite unmanifested
Consciousness of Oneness.

What does it feel like to become present to the Trinity Wombs in your body, feeling your direct connection with your Spiritual nature?

~ evolution of the Feminine Soul

~ evolution of the Feminine Soul

Day 4
Waxing Crescent Lunar Journey

I Align with My Inner Truth Within

~ evolution of the Feminine Soul

Fifth Pillar
Embodying our Sacred Feminine Form

Our physical body is Sacred; an expression of Divine Light which is further refracted into the *Universal Qualities of Love, Beauty, Compassion, Justice, Freedom,* etc. This light is experienced in our physical body through visceral embodiment. As women, collectively, we have objectified and diminished the value of our bodies for the sake of survival. It is time to change the collective story of our value and embrace the sacredness and beauty in our own Feminine form. Our bodies are a vessel housing the Great Spirit of Divine, Oneness… along with deep emotional intelligence, intuitive knowing, and the magical ability to transmit, transform and alchemize *Spirit.*

How does it feel to become present to the inherent perfection of your physical Feminine form, embracing the sacredness in your biology, emotional waves, intuitive awareness and mystery within?

~ evolution of the Feminine Soul

~ evolution of the Feminine Soul

Day 5
Waxing Crescent Lunar Journey

I Clarify My Deepest Intention

~ evolution of the Feminine Soul

Sixth Pillar
Healing the 3 Collective Wounds of the Feminine

The three core collective wounds of the Feminine have been stored unconsciously in our subtle fields, disrupting the three lower subtle body centers in women. This disruption has caused the great difficulty women have of embodying their divinity of the earthly, sensual nature of their physical body. Reclaiming our Feminine sacredness is key to embodying the Truth of who we are and healing the collective wounds of the Feminine.

1st **Collective Wound of the Feminine in the Solar Plexus: Powerlessness**
2nd **Collective Wound of the Feminine of the Sacral Womb: Shame**
3rd **Collective Wound of the Feminine of the Root Gate: Abandonment**

Begin by exploring your relationship with each one of these wounds in your life. This will begin the transformation and the *Sacred Initiation* in each center, respectively, as you reclaim your Feminine Soul from each.

1st **Sacred Initiation: Conscious Feminine Power**
2nd **Sacred Initiation: Conscious Feminine Body Wisdom**
3rd **Sacred Initiation: Conscious Feminine Union**

~ evolution of the Feminine Soul

1st Collective Wound of the Feminine
Powerlessness
Embodying Conscious Feminine Sacred Power
in your Solar Plexus Gateway

How do I feel about my Self… my identity?
How attached am I to my identity in the world?
Can I begin to experience a 'Me' that is not my behavior,
nor my roles, nor my emotions, nor my thoughts?
What does it feel to experience myself as
pure consciousness having a human experience?
Can I embrace my *Conscious Feminine Sacred Power* within?

~ evolution of the Feminine Soul

~ evolution of the Feminine Soul

2nd Collective Wound of the Feminine

Shame

Sacred Initiation of Conscious Feminine Body Wisdom in your Sacral Gateway

How do I feel about my body?
Do I feel shame about my body, sexuality, being a woman or any feminine quality (emotions, sensitivity, intuition etc.)?
Am I willing to step into the beauty, sacredness, purity and magnificence of my female form?

~ evolution of the Feminine Soul

~ evolution of the Feminine Soul

3rd Collective Wound of the Feminine
Abandonment
Sacred Initiation of Conscious Feminine Union
in your Root Gateway

Do I feel abandoned, disconnected or victimized in any way?
How safe do I feel in my body, on this Earth plane?
How does it feel to know that I am one with the Universe, and that my Essence is not separate, but one in the same with that of Source?
How does it feel to know that source has never abandoned me and it is not possible because I am that spark of divinity within?
Can I feel the connection of consciousness,
Herself, pulsing within me?

~ evolution of the Feminine Soul

~ evolution of the Feminine Soul

Day 6
Waxing Crescent Lunar Journey

I Envision My Heart's Desire

~ evolution of the Feminine Soul

Seventh Pillar
Transforming 1st World Feminine Disorders

Much of the dysfunction in women's physical bodies and psyches have been created by the cultural and religious repression of the Feminine, through many lifetimes in the last 5000 years. This has manifested as diseases, disorders and pervasive dissatisfaction in our lives.

The *1st world Feminine Dysfunction* is a category of physical imbalances that have resulted in 1st world countries due to this severance between spirit and body. They manifest in women as nervous disorders, reproductive disorders, auto-immune imbalances, gut imbalances, and emotional disorders.

Become present with your physical and emotional body... practice the art of listening deeply to the unresolved feelings underlying whichever imbalances are showing up in your body. Honoring the repressed emotions and allowing yourself to reclaim these rejected, judged and lost parts of you is key to unraveling these conditions and restoring health.

What physical or emotional imbalances have been challenging you? Let yourself sit in reflection and listen deeply to the underlying emotion that is calling out to be heard, acknowledged and seen. By listening to the body's messages, you allow these unresolved places of past pain to resolve themselves into the light of love and compassion of the Feminine.

Journal your feelings as you do this.

~ evolution of the Feminine Soul

~ evolution of the Feminine Soul

Day 7
Waxing Quarter Lunar Journey

I Am The Bridge, Birthing Consciousness

~ evolution of the Feminine Soul

Eighth Pillar
Embracing the Biochemistry of Consciousness

Our physical body is a manifestation of the interplay of the inner relationship of our subtle bodies; emotional body, mental body and spiritual body. Healing is a manifestation of bridging consciousness itself through the matter of substance, allowing the resolution of the illusion of separation to dissolve. Our presence (consciousness) and where we choose to focus it on, affects the biochemistry in our body. By becoming present to the constricted, painful places in our Being, our biochemistry shifts and releases the constrictions itself, thus healing occurs.

Contemplate your emotional, mental and soul body through Breath and Presence, bringing awareness and space to the reality that you are consciousness and it is living within you right now. How does it feel, what unwinds within?

~ evolution of the Feminine Soul

~ evolution of the Feminine Soul

Day 8
Waxing Gibbous Lunar Journey

I Honor My Sovereignty

~ evolution of the Feminine Soul

Ninth Pillar
Integrating the 5 Elemental Mothers

The five *Elemental MOTHERS*;
Earth, Water, Fire, Air & Ether (Consciousness)
are the sacred substance of all creation, including our own form.

Earth Mother... roots your Soul.
Ocean Mother of Love... dissolves you into Love.
Cosmic Womb Mother of Air... sustains you in Her Mystery.
Dragon Mother of Fire... awakens your Life Force.
Dark Moon Mother of Ether... annihilates you
into Her Primordial Essence.

~ evolution of the Feminine Soul

~ evolution of the Feminine Soul

Can you feel the Elemental Mothers alive within You?

Spend a few minutes breathing into these Elements. Notice how they shift what is happening in your body and consciousness. Remember that everything in your body has consciousness, including your organs and cells. Bring your awareness to the elements within and start noticing how you awaken to a whole new perspective. As you reflect and breathe in each organ you can allow old calcified emotional patterns of pain to dissolve.

~ evolution of the Feminine Soul

EARTH

Take a few minutes with the Earth Mother...
breathing in Trust, exhaling Worrying... activating your Earth
through your Stomach and Spleen.

~ evolution of the Feminine Soul

WATER

Take a few minutes with the Ocean Mother of Love,
breathing in Love and Safety, exhaling Fear... activating your Water
through your kidneys and bladder.

~ evolution of the Feminine Soul

FIRE

Take a few minutes with the Fire Mother of Dragons,
breathing in Joy, exhaling Anxiety, activating your Fire
through your heart, small intestine, pericardium and triple burner.

~ evolution of the Feminine Soul

AIR

Take a few minutes with the Cosmic Womb Mother of Air, breathing in Inspiration and releasing Grief, activating your Air through your lungs and large intestines.

~ evolution of the Feminine Soul

ETHER

Take a few minutes with the Ether Dark Moon Mother,
breathing in Vitality and exhaling Anger... activating your Ether
through your Liver and Gall Bladder.

~ evolution of the Feminine Soul

Day 9
Waxing Gibbous Lunar Journey

I Feel the Pulse of the Universe live within Me

~ evolution of the Feminine Soul

Tenth Pillar
Embracing Evolutionary Activations

Physical, emotional and spiritual crisis are evolutionary activations and opportunities for realization of our greatest potential, from our loving Universe.

At all moments, the Universe is conspiring to support us in manifesting our greatest potential… making sure we have everything we need, in order to expand into greater levels of Her Reality of Love.

Therefore, everything we experience including challenges, are out of Love… and it provides us with a map to break free from the wounds that bind us to painful illusions of separation. The challenges force you to relinquish the unconscious patterns of limitation. The key to transcending the challenge is to recognize the unconscious pattern that is operating within you that creates the challenge, by becoming aware of the emotions that arise in the situation.

Become present to the emotion that arises in your present challenge. Breathe with it and let yourself bring your conscious awareness to that unresolved part of you. Once you have done this, there is much more Light in your Being, and you can then sit quietly and ask for the guidance in this particular situation.

~ evolution of the Feminine Soul

Secondly, we can look back at the challenges in our lives, and reflect on what did it force you to see, experience, embody?

~ evolution of the Feminine Soul

Day 10
Waxing Gibbous Lunar Journey

I Feel the Deep Yearning of My Heart

~ evolution of the Feminine Soul

Eleventh Pillar
Embodying Consciousness of Movement in Stillness

We are embodied *Consciousness*, and *Consciousness* is constantly manifesting through our thoughts, emotions and actions. We are an extension and expression of the *Oneness Consciousness*, in the constant expression of *Movement in Stillness*.

Feeling the dance of movement in stillness allows us to awaken to the reality of oneness within two opposing states (duality); form and formlessness, yin and yang, which is a key element of restoring the rhythm in our being.

The rhythm of life reflects in the cyclic time of seasons, cycles of the moon, our menstrual cycle and our biological rhythms, regardless of our age. *Movement and Stillness* are key components in the dance of *Oneness*.

Consciously, observe the balance of Stillness and Movement in your life; are you in rhythm of being vs. doing, rest vs activity?

~ evolution of the Feminine Soul

~ evolution of the Feminine Soul

Day 11
Waxing Gibbous Lunar Journey

I Am the Dance of Light

~ evolution of the Feminine Soul

Twelfth Pillar
Activating the Sacred Initiations

Through the *Sacred Initiations of the Feminine*, we can heal our bodies, hearts, and souls and awaken the complete potential of the Feminine within us. We are living in a special time in which the Feminine is awakening on the planet through each one of us; we each represent a fractal aspect of the collective wounding. The *Sacred Initiations* are a transformational initiatory experience of the Feminine through consciousness, spiritual alchemy and embodiment on a personal level, thus affecting the collective level.

Are your ready to let go of the collective and personal wounds and experience your greatest brilliance?

~ evolution of the Feminine Soul

~ evolution of the Feminine Soul

Day 12
Waxing Gibbous Lunar Journey

I Am Movement in Stillness

~ evolution of the Feminine Soul

Thirteenth Pillar
Awakening to Oneness Realization

Reawakening our *Feminine Essence* within, in harmony with our Masculine qualities allows us to activate the template of the perfected human being; *Sophiatic Christos*, the marriage of our duality leading us into *Unity*.

In order to bring ourselves into the next evolutionary reality of *Unity* consciousness; where we can experience our Divine Nature in our physical body… we must reclaim the lost Feminine within and evolve our consciousness through Her. By resurrecting Her fierce compassion and unconditional love, we can create the union of opposites within us and thus transcend the plane of duality, moving into the domain of *Oneness*.

Let yourself feel the perfection in your Being and surrender everything you think you know, into this Light of your Soul.

~ evolution of the Feminine Soul

~ evolution of the Feminine Soul

Day 13
Waxing Gibbous Lunar Journey

I Express My Truth Unapologetically

~ evolution of the Feminine Soul

Conscious Feminine Manifesto

the Conscious Feminine within knows...
Knows **Her Power resides** within Herself.
Knows Her Truth is Love…. and that this is the Nature of Her Spirit.
Knows it is not about loving Herself, it's about knowing
She is the Love.

She…

Knows *True Freedom, Peace and Love are* within Her
and no one can take away who **She** is.
Knows Her Heart holds the key to Peace and Happiness, rather than
dependence on anyone or anything outside of Herself.
Knows **She** can Trust the Wisdom in Her Heart;
knowing exactly what is right action at all moments.
Knows Truth will set Her Free.

She…

Knows **She** is enough!
Knows **She** has the ability to Heal all aspects of Her body.
Knows **She** is an expression of Source.

~ evolution of the Feminine Soul

She...

Knows **She** carries all the Divine Qualities within Her
to be unfolded through Her Journey of Life.
Knows feelings of Fear, Anger, Resentment and otHer
intense emotions are experienced but do not determine who **She** is.
Knows **She** experiences thoughts and beliefs,
but knows this is not who **She** is.
Knows **She** is an endless source of Creativity.
Knows Love can Transform everything within Herself,
Her Family and Her World.

She...

Has Compassion and Mercy with Herself when **She** forgets Her Truth.
Knows Her Body is a reflection of what is happening on
the otHer subtle levels of emotions, mind, heart and soul.
Knows Her Body is the Vessel of Light
that Spirit creates Life through.
Knows in Her Sensitivity is the Secret of Her Intuition
and Connection with Source.

She...

Knows **She** carries a Jewel of Love in Her heart.
Knows Her Body is Sacred.
Knows Her Body is in tune with the wisdom of the cycles of nature.
Knows **She** doesn't have to do anything to be worthy,
She is already worthy.
Knows Wisdom is felt in Her Body, not in Her head.
Knows all of Life is Sacred and deserves respect.
Dares to express Herself fully with compassion and mercy to all.
Sees the Oneness in all of Us, and knows the beauty each
living person or thing carries.

~ evolution of the Feminine Soul

She...

Doesn't depend on the Ideas or the Feelings of others
to determine how **She** feels about herself.
Knows the pain and the suffering of the past can be transformed,
freeing Her to live Joyously in this moment.
Knows **She** is constantly loved & supported by the Cosmos,
Universe & Source of all Love.

She...

Knows Her worth is not dependent on any physical feature
but ratHer on the Truth of who **She** is; as the Source of Love.
Knows Her sexuality is sacred and is the force
of the Creation moving through Her Being.
Knows **She** is on a Journey, ultimately to be
the highest reflection of Love on the planet.

She...

Holds no judgment towards Herself, Her Sisters and Her Brothers,
knowing **She** has been in many dark places before.
Knows **She** has the power to change the world
through Her creativity.
Holds Her brothers and sisters in Oneness ratHer than competition.
Knows Abundance is Her True state.
Knows **She** is the message of Love.

~ evolution of the Feminine Soul

Day 14
Waxing Gibbous Lunar Journey

I Feel the Illumination of My Being

~ evolution of the Feminine Soul

What is your Conscious Feminine Manifesto?

Write your own Conscious Feminine Manifesto. Start with ones that resonate with you, from my previous list. Tune into your heart and see what else wants to express through you. Read them every morning as a gentle reminder to yourself.

~ evolution of the Feminine Soul

~ evolution of the Feminine Soul

Day 15
Full Moon Lunar Journey

I Am Exalted In My Unique Expression

~ evolution of the Feminine Soul

~ evolution of the Feminine Soul

The Waning Phase of the Moon

After the full moon, the light of the moon begins to dissolve as She turns inward, reflecting, distilling and preparing for a new birth. Take the opportunity to reflect on these key words of her wisdom, as you turn your focus inward and reap the wisdom of the waning phase of the moon.

~ evolution of the Feminine Soul

Day 16
Waning Gibbous Lunar Journey

I Am an Expression of Consciousness, Herself

~ evolution of the Feminine Soul

~ evolution of the Feminine Soul

Day 17
Waning Gibbous Lunar Journey

I Am Love

~ evolution of the Feminine Soul

~ evolution of the Feminine Soul

Day 18
Waning Gibbous Lunar Journey

Compassion Becomes Alive through Me

~ evolution of the Feminine Soul

~ evolution of the Feminine Soul

Day 19
Waning Gibbous Lunar Journey

I Honor the Sacred Vessel of My Feminine Body

~ evolution of the Feminine Soul

~ evolution of the Feminine Soul

Day 20
Waning Gibbous Lunar Journey

I Welcome Transformation

~ evolution of the Feminine Soul

~ evolution of the Feminine Soul

Day 21
Waning Gibbous Lunar Journey

I Surrender My Head to My Heart

~ evolution of the Feminine Soul

~ evolution of the Feminine Soul

Day 22
Waning Quarter Lunar Journey

I Transcend into Not Knowing

~ evolution of the Feminine Soul

~ evolution of the Feminine Soul

Day 23
Waning Crescent Lunar Journey

I Align to the Rhythm of My Breath

~ evolution of the Feminine Soul

~ evolution of the Feminine Soul

Day 24
Waning Crescent Lunar Journey

I Return to the Wisdom of my Womb

~ evolution of the Feminine Soul

~ evolution of the Feminine Soul

Day 25
Waning Crescent Lunar Journey

I Listen to the Whisper of My Soul

~ evolution of the Feminine Soul

~ evolution of the Feminine Soul

Day 26
Waning Crescent Lunar Journey

I Dissolve into Essence

~ evolution of the Feminine Soul

~ evolution of the Feminine Soul

The Dark Moon Retreat Phase

Beginning on the 27th day, the Moon enters Her dissolution phase of death, becoming completely empty, in order to receive the light of the new cycle, on the New Moon.

Take these three days, to turn completely inward in retreat, surrendering the challenges and pain of the previous month, in order to create space for a new birth of your greatest Light.

~ evolution of the Feminine Soul

~ evolution of the Feminine Soul

Day 27
Dark Lunar Retreat

I Die to My Past

~ evolution of the Feminine Soul

~ evolution of the Feminine Soul

Day 28
Dark Lunar Retreat

I Merge with Oneness

~ evolution of the Feminine Soul

~ evolution of the Feminine Soul

Day 29

Dark Lunar Retreat

I Am No-Thing

~ evolution of the Feminine Soul

~ evolution of the Feminine Soul

The New Moon

Your Feminine Lunar Cycle begins anew, bringing forth new understandings, new wisdom and greater embodiment of Light. You are not the same person you were 30 days ago… you have transformed and transcended limiting beliefs and reclaimed your Feminine Soul into wholeness.

You are now poised at the beginning of a new cycle. The Feminine Lunar Cycle invites you for another round of creativity. What will you create, what will you let die, and what dream will you weave forth into creation?

You have been given another opportunity to dance in the creation of form… in your feminine body… upon this planet. What new possibility is yearning to be birthed through you this month? What greatness will you give expression to? All realms of possibility await you… as you begin anew, born out of No-Thing; that which gives birth to all is giving birth through you.

Dream your greatest dream!

~ evolution of the Feminine Soul

New Moon

A New Creation Awaits Me

~ evolution of the Feminine Soul

~ evolution of the Feminine Soul

An Invocation to Great Mother

I bow my head, heart and womb to you.

For you are the Creator & Created.

From your womb, the ten thousands things are born.

I ask that you bring me close to you,

keep me in your flow of Divine Grace.

Hold me in our ecstatic presence where all veils are dissolved…

Leaving only your whispering Truth as my Teacher.

Let me drink from your cup and merge with you

into the annihilation of our Being,

forever and ever!

~ Leonor Murciano Luna

~ evolution of the Feminine Soul

~ evolution of the Feminine Soul

May *Light and Love*

be your *experience*

everyday

& may you remember the

Truth of LOVE

that is *YOU!*

~ evolution of the Feminine Soul

~ evolution of the Feminine Soul

Leonor Murciano, PhD, IMD, AP is an Integrative physician, Acupuncture Physician, Author, Spiritual Healer and Teacher. She is the founder of *Nourishing Women Center*, the *School of Conscious Feminine Medicine* and *W.O.W. Generation – (Women of Wisdom)* non-for profit organization serving adolescent girls.

Dr. Murciano embarked on a profound healing journey when unexpectedly she began to re-call and re-experience old traumatic memories of a near-death-experience she had at the age of 6 1/2. These visceral memories triggered a profound healing crisis biologically, emotionally and psycho-spiritually. This intense, transformational healing journey inspired her work, carving out a very distinct healing map which has become the foundation of the *School of Conscious Feminine Medicine*, dedicated to the healing of women on the planet.

Author of:
Feminine Wisdom: Rise of a New Creation, a guidebook of wholistic medicine for those challenged with Infertility.
Evolution of the Feminine Soul, ~a transformational journal for women awakening to the Feminine.
Birth of the Conscious Feminine, coming in (2019), encompassing the principles of Conscious Feminine Medicine.

More importantly, Dr. Murciano is the mother of three beautiful young women, each thriving in their own unique way. She continues to write, teach, mentor and attend to patients in South Florida.

For more information and upcoming events, please visit her website, ConsciousFeminineMedicine.com.

~ evolution of the Feminine Soul

Made in United States
North Haven, CT
18 October 2023